*[Hannibal] was by far the [best soldier]
both of the cavalry and the infantry,
the first to enter the fight and the last to leave the field. But
these great merits were matched by great vices—inhuman
cruelty . . . and an utter absence of truthfulness, reverence,
fear of the gods, respect for oaths, sense of religion.*

Livy, Roman historian,
circa. 20 B.C.

ೞೞೞೞೞೞೞೞ

Hannibal Barca was the sworn enemy of Rome,
one of the most powerful nations on earth. He
ransacked the Roman countryside, leaving fields in
ruins and villages in flames. But was Hannibal truly
wicked? Or were his tactics the same as those used
by his enemies? Gather the evidence as you read and
decide for yourself!

*For Jordi Artigas and Nina Artigas. Two of my favorite people.*

Photographs ©: akg-images: 48, 55 (Peter Connolly), 53, 62 bottom (Heinrich Leutemann), 64 bottom, 96 (R. Weibezahl); Alamy Images: 17, 60 top (Gordon Sinclair), 18, 21, 60 bottom, 61 top, 136, 137 (North Wind Picture Archives), 32 (Peter Horree), 39, 58, 65 bottom, 108 (Mary Evans Picture Library), 60 center (Visual Arts Library, London), 87 (Ivy Close Images); Ancient Art & Architecture Collection Ltd./Prisma: 99; Bridgeman Images: 25, 57, 62 top, 64 center, 102, 112 (Look and Learn), 74 (Alinari); Corbis Images: 61 bottom (Michael Busselle), 65 center, 115 (Bettmann); Getty Images: 46 (Spencer Arnold), 61 center (Hulton Archive), 64 top (Time Life Pictures/Mansell/The LIFE Picture Collection); Mary Evans Picture Library: 81; The Granger Collection, New York: 10, 65 top, 119 (ullstein bild); The Image Works: 36 (The British Library/Topham), 63 top, 72, 73 (Pietro Baguzzi/akg-images), 63 bottom, 90 (North Wind Picture Archives), 84 (Roger-Viollet); Shutterstock: 123, 125, 127 (veronchick84), 132 (BM Design), 22 border, 38, 39 border, 74 border, 122 (Waj)

**Illustrations by XNR Productions, Inc.: 4, 5, 8, 9, 22**
**Cover art, page 8 inset by Mark Summers**
**Chapter art by Raphael Montoliu**

Library of Congress Cataloging-in-Publication Data
Brooks, Philip, 1963-
Hannibal : Rome's worst nightmare / by Philip Brooks. — Revised edition.
pages cm. — (A wicked history)
Includes bibliographical references and index.
ISBN 978-0-531-22122-8 (library binding) — ISBN 978-0-531-22330-7 (pbk.)
1. Hannibal, 247 B.C.-182 B.C.—Juvenile literature. 2. Punic War, 2nd, 218-201 B.C.—Juvenile literature. 3. Generals—Tunisia—Carthage (Extinct city)—Biography—Juvenile literature. 4. Rome—History—Republic, 265-30 B.C.—Juvenile literature. 5. Carthage (Extinct city)—History—Juvenile literature. I. Title.
DG249.B77 2015
937'.04092—dc23
[B]
2015019350

**Tod Olson, Series Editor**
**Marie O'Neill, Art Director**
**Allicette Torres, Cover Design**
**SimonSays Design!, Book Design and Production**

© 2016, 2009 Scholastic Inc.

1 2 3 4 5 6 7 8 9 10 R 25 24 23 22 21 20 19 18 17 16

# Hannibal

## Rome's Worst Nightmare

PHILIP BROOKS

Franklin Watts®
An Imprint of Scholastic Inc.
New York Toronto London Auckland Sydney
Mexico City New Delhi Hong Kong
Danbury, Connecticut

# The World of Hannibal

As commander of the army of Carthage, Hannibal battled
Rome for control of the Mediterranean world.

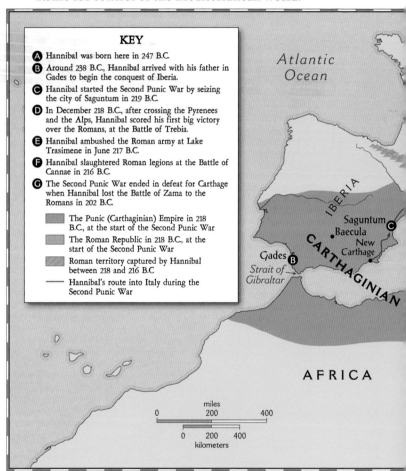

### KEY

**A** Hannibal was born here in 247 B.C.

**B** Around 238 B.C., Hannibal arrived with his father in Gades to begin the conquest of Iberia.

**C** Hannibal started the Second Punic War by seizing the city of Saguntum in 219 B.C.

**D** In December 218 B.C., after crossing the Pyrenees and the Alps, Hannibal scored his first big victory over the Romans, at the Battle of Trebia.

**E** Hannibal ambushed the Roman army at Lake Trasimene in June 217 B.C.

**F** Hannibal slaughtered Roman legions at the Battle of Cannae in 216 B.C.

**G** The Second Punic War ended in defeat for Carthage when Hannibal lost the Battle of Zama to the Romans in 202 B.C.

The Punic (Carthaginian) Empire in 218 B.C., at the start of the Second Punic War

The Roman Republic in 218 B.C., at the start of the Second Punic War

Roman territory captured by Hannibal between 218 and 216 B.C

— Hannibal's route into Italy during the Second Punic War

Atlantic
Ocean

IBERIA

Saguntum **C**
Baecula
New
Gades **B** Carthage
Strait of
Gibraltar

CARTHAGINIAN

AFRICA

miles
0    200        400

0    200   400
kilometers

# TABLE OF CONTENTS

# A Wicked Web

A look at the allies and enemies of Hannibal.

## Family and Friends

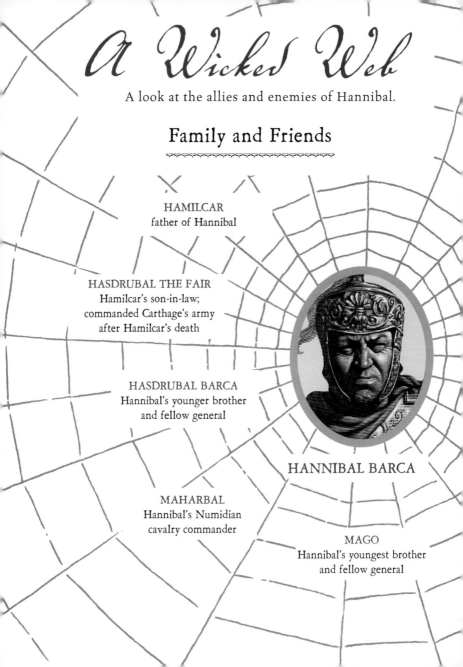

**HAMILCAR**
father of Hannibal

**HASDRUBAL THE FAIR**
Hamilcar's son-in-law;
commanded Carthage's army
after Hamilcar's death

**HASDRUBAL BARCA**
Hannibal's younger brother
and fellow general

**HANNIBAL BARCA**

**MAHARBAL**
Hannibal's Numidian
cavalry commander

**MAGO**
Hannibal's youngest brother
and fellow general

# Fighters

∽∽∽∽∽∽∽∽∽∽∽

**LIBYAN INFANTRY**
expert foot soldiers from
North Africa

**NUMIDIAN CAVALRY**
elite North African horsemen

**CELTS OF
NORTHERN SPAIN**

**GAULS OF FRANCE AND
NORTHERN ITALY**

**IBERIANS OF
SOUTHERN SPAIN**

tribes whose men were conquered and drafted by Hannibal

# Enemies

∽∽∽∽∽∽∽∽∽∽∽

**SCIPIO**
first Roman consul to
face Hannibal; led Roman
forces in Iberia

**FABIUS**
dictator nicknamed "The
Delayer" for his passive
tactics against Hannibal

**FLAMINIUS**
Roman consul who fought
Hannibal at Lake Trasimene

**VARRO AND PAULLUS**
Roman consuls who fought
Hannibal at Cannae

**SEMPRONIUS**
Roman consul who fought
Hannibal at Lake Trebia

**SCIPIO AFRICANUS**
elder Scipio's son;
fought Hannibal at Zama

**HANNO**
leader of Hannibal's
opponents in Carthage

HANNIBAL BARCA, 247–183 B.C.

ON A SUMMER DAY IN 217 B.C. A SHOCKING
rumor spread through the markets, streets, and temples
of Rome. Was it true there had been a terrible defeat?
Had tens of thousands of Roman soldiers really been
killed or captured?

Frantic mothers and fathers begged military leaders
in the city for word of their sons. Women and children
wept, fearing they had lost their husbands and fathers.

Finally, a crowd gathered in the Forum, Rome's
central square. The crowd rushed to the Senate House,
where the city's leaders were meeting in emergency
session. The anxious citizens pounded at the doors until
a senator finally stepped outside. Silence fell while the
senator announced the truth to the crowd. "We have
been defeated in a great battle," he declared.

It took days for the full effects of the disaster to
become known. At Lake Trasimene, a few hundred

miles to the north, a mighty invading army had indeed slaughtered tens of thousands of Rome's best soldiers. Their corpses had been dragged into great piles and burned, filling the air with terrible smoke. Thousands more had been cut down in the water while trying to swim to safety. The lake turned red with the blood of Roman soldiers.

The name of the man responsible for the bloodshed passed through the crowd that day like a cold wind. He was Hannibal Barca, the fearsome military leader from Carthage.

Carthage, center of the great Punic Empire, was Rome's archenemy from the other side of the Mediterranean Sea. A year earlier, Hannibal had dragged his army across two mountain ranges and driven it into the heart of the Roman Republic. He had ravaged crops and looted villages to feed his hungry troops. He had won massive battles against the Roman army, one of the best-trained fighting forces on earth.

Now, Hannibal was marching south toward Rome.

The Roman senators scrambled to plan for the republic's defense. They called for a dictator to direct military operations. The new leader sent out men to destroy bridges on the route to Rome. He ordered the city's walls and towers strengthened.

Meanwhile, Romans prayed to their gods for help. Priests searched for omens of good fortune or bad. Some even offered human sacrifices in the hope that it would please the gods.

For Hannibal, the terror he instilled in the Romans was a dream come true. As a boy, he had sworn to battle Rome until his dying breath. Now, he was pursuing his mission with ruthless determination.

It was a battle to the death between the world's two most powerful military forces. If Hannibal won, Carthage would control the vital Mediterranean Sea and all the lands around it. Rome would become an outpost in the Punic Empire. If he lost, once-mighty Carthage would be squashed by the Roman Republic.

*Consider these questions as you read about Hannibal's early life.*

**BIG QUESTION:**

How was Hannibal groomed to be a military leader?

**RELATED QUESTIONS:**

- Why were the Carthaginians and the Romans sworn enemies?

- What promise did Hannibal make to his father in the temple?

- Describe Hannibal's army.

# PART 1

# The Making of a Commander

# Hamilcar's Son

A general's boy swears to OPPOSE
HIS FATHER'S ARCHENEMY.

Hannibal was born in 247 B.C. in the
city of Carthage. His father, Hamilcar Barca, was no
doubt proud to have a son, an heir to his fortune. But
Hamilcar had little time to enjoy fatherhood. Carthage
was at war, and as one of its most trusted military
commanders, he had to defend the empire.

At the time, the Punic Empire was one of the most
advanced powers in the world. Its biggest city, Carthage,
was home to about 400,000 people. It stood at the tip
of North Africa on the shore of the Mediterranean Sea.

Surrounded by massive walls and two soaring towers, the city overlooked two busy harbors. One harbor provided a wharf for trading ships, which brought a constant stream of gold, silver, textiles, and spices to the city's wealthy merchants. The other harbor sheltered Carthage's powerful navy, which was locked in a battle for control over the waters of the Mediterranean.

AT ITS PEAK, CARTHAGE WAS the most powerful city in the known world. Its navy dominated the Mediterranean Sea. But in the third century B.C., its empire was threatened by the expanding Roman Republic.

At the time of Hannibal's birth, the Carthaginian military was stretched to its limits. The Roman Republic, which lay across the Mediterranean in present-day Italy, had been challenging Carthage for 17 years in the First Punic War. In 247 B.C., all eyes were on Sicily, an island off the southern coast of Italy. Roman forces were on the move there. If they took control of Sicily, the Roman navy would control the trade routes of the Mediterranean.

Before Hannibal's first birthday, Hamilcar Barca loaded his soldiers on ships and sailed across to Sicily. He was greatly outnumbered by the Romans, who maintained a disciplined and well-trained army with countless reinforcements. But Hamilcar fought with intelligence and ferocity. The war dragged on for years.

HAMILCAR BARCA, Hannibal's father, was the greatest Carthaginian general of his day.

Finally, when Hannibal was six years old, the balance tipped in Rome's favor. In 241 B.C., Carthage sent a fleet of 170 ships to supply Hamilcar with weapons, food, and reinforcements. Roman warships intercepted the Carthaginian fleet west of Sicily. The Romans used their unique "corvus," or assault bridge, to great effect. The bridge swiveled out over the sea onto enemy vessels. Roman soldiers then stormed across and slaughtered their foes in hand-to-hand combat. Only 50 Carthaginian warships survived the battle. The ravaged fleet retreated home, leaving Hamilcar with no choice but to negotiate for peace.

After 23 years of fighting, the First Punic War finally came to an end. Hamilcar was considered a hero, but he did not feel like one. The mighty Punic Empire had been humiliated. In exchange for peace, Carthage paid Rome a huge sum of money and gave up claims to the island of Sicily. Within three years, the Romans had taken over two more Mediterranean islands, Sardinia and Corsica.

Hamilcar was left to wait and plot his revenge. The sea now lay under the control of the Roman navy. Hamilcar would have to attack by land. He decided he would take an army across the sea to Iberia (present-day Spain and Portugal). Hamilcar would build a base in Iberia and recruit new soldiers. When he was ready, he would attack Rome.

Young Hannibal, meanwhile, spent his days learning Greek poetry and philosophy. But legend has it that he was drawn to his father's struggle while just a boy.

When he was nine years old, Hannibal supposedly found his father standing solemnly before a temple altar. Oil lamps cast flickering shadows over the walls. Hannibal listened as the priest told his father that the gods looked favorably upon his upcoming expedition.

Hannibal asked his father where he was going. Hamilcar explained that he was leading an army to Iberia, and Hannibal begged to join his father on the adventure.

Hamilcar thought for a moment, and then asked his son to stand beside him. "Swear to be always an enemy of Rome," he commanded.

Hannibal met his father's gaze. "I swear to be always an enemy of Rome," he said.

"I SWEAR TO BE ALWAYS AN ENEMY OF ROME." That's the vow that Hannibal took when he was a child. His father, Hamilcar, was still determined to crush Rome. Having lost control of the Mediterranean, Hamilcar planned to attack by land from a base in Europe.

# THE WORLD OF THE FIRST PUNIC WAR

DURING HANNIBAL'S TIME, EUROPEAN AND African nations as they are known today did not exist. The Punic Empire ruled over much of North Africa. Across the Mediterranean, Rome held southern Italy and the Mediterranean islands of Sicily, Sardinia, and Corsica.

The lands that now make up Spain and France were dominated by small independent tribes. These tribes were too weak to resist the military might of Rome or Carthage. Southern Spain was divided among tribes of people known as Iberians. Northern Spain was home to the Celts, who had moved there from present-day Great Britain. Farther north, the Gauls lived in present-day France and northern Italy.

Men from all three tribes would soon become foot soldiers in the second great war for control of the Mediterranean world.

ROME AND CARTHAGE
dominated the ancient
Mediterranean world.

# CHAPTER 2

# Iberian Training

## Hannibal learns to be A SOLDIER AND A MAN.

NOT LONG AFTER HANNIBAL SWORE HIS solemn oath against the Romans, he followed his father out of Carthage.

Hamilcar had led the Carthaginian army west along the northern coast of Africa. In the center marched the infantry, thousands of foot soldiers in a long column with their shields glinting in the sun. To either side rode the cavalry atop well-groomed horses. Hundreds of pack animals trudged behind, carrying food and supplies. Somewhere in the procession, dozens of battle elephants plodded along, trained to batter enemy lines like primitive tanks.

Slowly, the army made its way toward the Strait of Gibraltar, where it would make a short sea journey to Iberia. Along the way, Hannibal's father met with village leaders, many of whom contributed soldiers and supplies.

Finally, the army boarded ships and made the crossing. They headed for the trading city of Gades on the Iberian coast. A Carthaginian ally, Gades would become Hamilcar's base.

No one knows when young Hannibal started fighting with his father's army. But he saw a lot of action over the next ten years. Slowly, Hamilcar's army swept through southern Iberia, conquering bands of Iberians and Celts. His men swung swords and flung spears, javelins, and rocks. Battles were bloody. There was little medical care for wounded men. A nasty cut or broken bone could be fatal.

The Celts and Iberians had similar weapons, but they failed to unite against the Carthaginians. Fighting

A CARTHAGINIAN GENERAL commands his troops from atop a war elephant. For ten years Hamilcar's army fought battles to bring Spanish tribes under the control of the Punic Empire.

in small groups, they didn't stand a chance. Defeated chiefs often met a gruesome end. Hamilcar had them nailed to crosses as examples to others. Men who could be trusted were brought into the Carthaginian army. Those who could not were enslaved.

In 228 B.C., when Hannibal was 19 years old, his father's long military career came to an end. According to one story, Hamilcar died while protecting Hannibal and another son from a surprise attack organized by a local chief called Orissus. Hamilcar is said to have sent his sons away on horseback while he led the attackers on a chase across a river. Swept off his horse, he was carried downriver and drowned.

Hannibal mourned his father's death. At the same time, he had been taught to believe that sacrifice was part of the life of a noble warrior. He had grown up believing that the powerful Barca family was meant to serve the glory of Carthage. Hannibal might have thought back to the oath he'd sworn ten years before. For a moment, he likely considered that he would end up like his father one day, a soldier killed in battle. So be it. His father had lived and died an enemy of Rome and so would he.

# CHAPTER 3

# War Must Go On

Hannibal's brother-in-law takes over
and BUILDS A KINGDOM.

HANNIBAL MAY HAVE BEEN EAGER TO
take command of the army—but he was not yet ready.
His brother-in-law, Hasdrubal the Fair, took over
instead. Hannibal watched and learned as Hasdrubal
extended the Punic Empire's control over Iberia.

Carthage's new army commander was handsome,
smart, and brutal. He began his command by avenging
Hamilcar's death. With a force of more than 50,000,
Hasdrubal slaughtered the chief Orissus and any of the
chief's followers he could find.

Hasdrubal followed this display of brute force with skillful diplomacy. He met with the southern chieftains who were still independent. He offered them protection from the Celts in the north if they pledged their loyalty to Carthage. Most of them agreed, bringing new soldiers into the army without costly fighting.

Hasdrubal and his men then built a city on the eastern shore of Iberia. They called it New Carthage. It quickly became a trading center filled with soldiers and merchants. The city had an excellent harbor. Nearby forests provided the huge supply of timber needed to rebuild Carthage's navy. Rich mines produced piles of silver to send home to Carthage. Hasdrubal built himself a palace and ruled southern Iberia as a king. He even minted silver coins with his own image on them.

Across the Mediterranean, the leaders of the Punic Empire viewed New Carthage with mixed feelings. They were happy to see the empire extended. But the Barca family's ambition worried some senators. Hasdrubal had grown powerful and hard to control. His aggression toward Rome brought back bad memories from the First Punic War. If Rome was angered, Carthage could be completely destroyed.

But Hasdrubal's success caused even more anxiety in Rome. In 226 B.C., Roman ambassadors arrived in New Carthage to negotiate the fate of Iberia. The two sides agreed that Carthage would control all of southern Iberia—except the city of Saguntum, which was already allied with Rome. The Roman Republic would control the north.

Once again, Hannibal had watched Hasdrubal achieve his goals through diplomacy. Hasdrubal knew he was not yet strong enough to fight the Romans. He needed time to bring supplies and soldiers to Iberia. In the meantime, peace with Rome would make the Mediterranean safe for Carthage's merchant ships.

During his seven years under Hasdrubal's command, Hannibal also learned how to fight. In small battles with Iberian and Celtic tribesmen, he proved himself agile and strong. He stayed calm in the heat of battle. He became Hasdrubal's most trusted lieutenant.

According to Titus Livy, a famous Roman historian, the young lieutenant Hannibal reminded soldiers of the great hero Hamilcar. "They saw the same strength in [Hannibal's] face and gleam in his eye. . . . And neither did the soldiers feel more confidence and boldness under any other leader."

Hannibal's ability to command would soon be tested. One night in 221 B.C., a Celtic assassin slipped past several guards and killed Hasdrubal in his bed. Hannibal's training had come to an end.

C H A P T E R   4

# A New Leader

Hannibal is chosen and quickly
BREAKS THE PEACE
WITH ROME.

$W$ITH HASDRUBAL DEAD, GOVERNMENT
leaders in Carthage sent word that the soldiers
themselves should determine who would take
his place. When the soldiers were assembled,
Hannibal's name was immediately shouted out. A
huge cheer rang through the ranks. Carthaginians,
Celts, Iberians, and North African tribesman
all stamped their feet and banged their shields
in support.

AT THE AGE OF 26, HANNIBAL assumed control
of the Carthaginian army. His first move was to strike
Saguntum, an Iberian city allied with Rome.

So, by popular demand, Hannibal Barca took command of the army of New Carthage. He was 26 years old at the time. No one knows for sure what he looked like. Being of North African descent, his skin would probably have been dark. By all accounts, he was a powerfully built man. Something in his attitude inspired confidence among his men and fear in his enemies.

Hannibal stood and assured his soldiers that together they would enjoy many victories. His words were translated into the various languages of his soldiers and passed throughout the assembled army.

Hannibal, however, had more on his mind than speeches. He immediately sought to strengthen Carthage's alliance with the tribes of Spain. He married Imilce, the daughter of a powerful tribal leader. Little is known about her. She would barely see her husband in the years to come.

With his men in high spirits, Hannibal immediately went to war. The army marched out of New Carthage.

They moved into the highlands northwest of their capital. In two years of fighting, they scored hard-won victories against several tribes, expanding Carthage's power into the center of Iberia.

Then, ignoring his brother-in-law's treaty and warnings from Rome, Hannibal led thousands of cheering soldiers to Saguntum. In the spring of 219 B.C., they laid siege to the city. They set up battering rams to break through the city walls and catapults to hurl stones over them. Again and again, Hannibal sent his men racing at the city walls. Roman arrows, javelins, and stones rained down on them. Losses were heavy, and Hannibal had to settle in and wait.

Meanwhile, Rome sent an angry delegation to Carthage. The Roman ambassadors stood before the Carthaginian Senate and demanded to know whether its members had approved Hannibal's attack on Saguntum.

Finally, a Roman ambassador gave the Carthaginian Senate a choice: Send Hannibal to Rome in chains, or

Rome would attack. "We bring you war or peace," the ambassador said, "take which you please."

The senators signaled their answer with a defiant shout. Carthage would never hand over its commanding general to Rome.

The Roman ambassador left the Senate knowing that his efforts had failed. The Second Punic War was about to begin.

At least one member of the Senate felt that Carthage had just sealed its own fate. When the Romans had left, Hanno, the leading opponent of the Barcas, stood up and complained about Hannibal. "I feel nothing but loathing and detestation for the youth who is kindling this war," he said to the senators. "He ought to be sent to the farthest corner of the earth . . . where it would be impossible for him to disturb the welfare and tranquility of our State."

But in Iberia, Hannibal's war machine was moving too fast to stop. Late in the year, his men broke through

HANNIBAL ON HORSEBACK. His siege against the city
of Saguntum enraged the Romans. They demanded that Carthage
turn him over. The Carthaginian Senate was angry at Hannibal for
breaking the peace but refused to sacrifice him.

Saguntum's defenses and poured into the city. Many of its inhabitants made bonfires with their possessions and leaped into the flames rather than face Hannibal's brutal soldiers. The army killed thousands of Saguntines and stole anything of value.

Hannibal saw to it that his men were well paid and sent the rest of the spoils to Carthage. He sent most of his Iberian soldiers home to rest for the winter. As the men bid Hannibal farewell, they could hardly have imagined his plans for the spring.

# HANNIBAL'S MEN

THE ARMY THAT HANNIBAL COMMANDED during the Second Punic War was a truly international force. His troops were mostly mercenaries, paid soldiers from territories conquered by or allied with the Punic Empire. These men spoke many different languages and shared few customs.

The North African kingdom of Numidia supplied Hannibal with the best cavalry in the world. Numidians rode without saddles or bridles. Wielding javelins and spears, they rode in formation, making sudden turns on the battlefield to confuse the enemy.

The Balearic Islands off the coast of Spain gave Hannibal thousands of slingers. They used two types of slings to deadly effect. One allowed them to hurl stones long distances into a mass of enemy troops. Another allowed for sharp shooting at closer range. They were a rowdy bunch known for their enthusiastic looting of conquered towns.

The Celts and Iberians of Spain provided many tough foot soldiers. They were experienced fighters who used short swords to cut and slash. The tribes also provided cavalry that rode two soldiers to a horse. In battle, one soldier quickly dismounted to fight on the ground.

From Libya, Hannibal got thousands of steadfast and deadly infantry. Hannibal had absolute confidence in their training and discipline. He used them for massive assaults as well as for much smaller guerrilla operations.

In Italy, Hannibal would later recruit thousands of Gauls to join the infantry. Ancient enemies of Rome, they fought without armor, carried long swords for slashing, and were vicious attackers. But in a long battle, they often lost resolve to fight. For this reason, Hannibal generally sent them into enemy lines first and backed them up with the Libyans.

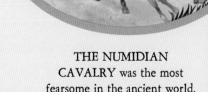

THE NUMIDIAN CAVALRY was the most fearsome in the ancient world.

*Consider these questions as you read about how Hannibal accomplished one of the greatest feats in military history.*

**BIG QUESTION:**

How did Hannibal's march to Rome exemplify his strengths as a military commander?

**RELATED QUESTIONS:**

- Why did Hannibal decide to invade Italy via a land route?

- How did Hannibal use his wits to outsmart the Volcae and the Allobroges?

- What did Hannibal's army endure when they crossed the Alps? What were the losses?

# PART 2

# The Journey of Death

# Chapter 5

# To Rome!

## Hannibal begins a long
## MARCH INTO THE MOUNTAINS.

HANNIBAL'S ARMY REASSEMBLED AT NEW
Carthage in the spring of 218 B.C. Word had arrived
from Carthage: They were officially at war with the
Roman Republic. Hannibal was eager to take the fight
to Rome, and in his mind there was only one route
available. Rome's navy controlled the seas; he would
have to march into Italy by land.

Hannibal's soldiers must have thought their
commander was crazy. It was 1,500 miles from New
Carthage to Rome. First, they would have to travel

through dangerous and little-known parts of northern Iberia. Then they would climb over two soaring, snow-covered mountain ranges—the Pyrenees and the Alps. It would be one of the most daring military feats ever attempted—or perhaps the most foolish.

But Hannibal was determined as he prepared for the journey. He had his men gather massive amounts of food and supplies. He sent scouts into northern Iberia to find the best routes and try to gain the support of local chieftains. The most powerful of the chiefs were paid to ensure the army safe passage. It was decided that Hannibal's brother Hasdrubal Barca would stay behind with 17,500 men to guard New Carthage.

In April, Hannibal led 90,000 infantry, 12,000 cavalry, and a few dozen elephants out of New Carthage and headed for the Pyrenees Mountains. They marched northward in a column that stretched for five miles. It was a massive force, but Hannibal knew that many would be lost to battle, disease, and exhaustion by the time they reached Italy.

The soldiers were racing against time. They had to cross the Pyrenees quickly and reach the towering Alps before early snows blocked their passage. With Hannibal driving them, they covered about 12 miles a day.

Along the way, Hannibal encountered resistance from several villages. His men fought fiercely and conquered each one. After each battle, Hannibal left soldiers behind to secure the villages.

Throughout the summer, word spread among the Iberians and Celts that the invaders and their general were invincible. As Hannibal swept north and east, many tribes began to believe he was a kind of god. Many of his men, too, came to believe he was divinely inspired. Their belief only strengthened their loyalty to Hannibal.

But that loyalty would be sorely tested during the hardships ahead.

# CHAPTER 6

# Battle on the Rhone

A sneak attack gets Hannibal out of a jam, but THE ROMANS ARE IN HOT PURSUIT.

IN THE LATE SUMMER OF 218 B.C., HANNIBAL and his men reached the foothills of the Pyrenees at the eastern edge of Iberia. At least 10,000 of his soldiers were dead. More than 10,000 others had been left behind to defend newly conquered territory. Thousands more had deserted. The 50,000 infantry,

9,000 cavalry, and 37 elephants that remained formed an experienced and deadly fighting unit.

Before climbing the Pyrenees, the army rested beside the sunny Mediterranean. They bathed in the blue water and ate well. When Hannibal gave the order, they trudged into the mountains. Snow lay on the peaks, but the summer weather allowed for easy hiking. With a few bribes and minor skirmishes, the mountain tribes

AS HANNIBAL MARCHED toward the Alps, he met with local tribes to ask for their support. Here, he meets with Gallic chieftains in southern France.

let them pass. When the army descended the slopes into southwestern Gaul—present-day France—they were in good spirits.

The arrival of a huge army caused alarm and hostility among the local Gauls. Hannibal called a meeting with several chieftains and won permission to pass without a fight. But when the army reached the banks of the Rhone River two weeks later, they found a surprise waiting for them. A Gallic tribe called the Volcae had gathered on the opposite shore. And they did not look friendly.

Hannibal formed a plan. He paid local tribesmen to build rafts for his troops. Then he sent a party of Iberian infantry and cavalry to cross secretly upriver. While he waited for them to get in position, his Gallic soldiers carved crude canoes from tree trunks. As Hannibal prepared his army, he made sure the Volcae could see his men prepare for the crossing.

Almost a week after arriving at the river's edge, Hannibal saw the signal he was waiting for. A column of white smoke rose in the distance to let him know the

HANNIBAL'S WAR ELEPHANTS CROSS the Rhone
River. Elephants fear water, so Hannibal had his men lead the
beasts onto rafts covered with soil.

48

Iberian party he had sent upriver was ready to sweep down on the Volcae in a surprise attack. He ordered the first canoes into the water. The men paddled their boats against the current. Cavalry horses and pack animals swam alongside them.

The Volcae swarmed out of their camp to occupy the beach, shouting and waving swords and spears.

As Hannibal's army paddled toward the shore, they saw their general's plan go into action. A portion of the Iberian cavalry he had sent upriver stormed the Volcae camp and set fire to it. The fire drew many of the Volcae away from the river. At that moment, the rest of Hannibal's ambushers rushed down onto the beach. Carthaginians and Volcae hacked at one another with short swords.

The first wave of paddling soldiers soon landed their boats and charged into the fight. Hit from two directions, the Volcae broke ranks and ran for their lives. Hannibal's cheering soldiers welcomed wave after wave of crossing comrades until darkness fell.

Celebration in the commanders' tent was short-lived. Hannibal's scouts informed him that a sizable Roman army had arrived at the mouth of the Rhone, four days ride to the south. Hannibal immediately sent 500 Numidian cavalry to scout the enemy.

The Roman army belonged to a consul, or leader, named Publius Scipio. Scipio had set sail from Italy with plans to confront Hannibal in Iberia. When Scipio docked in Gaul to load supplies, local Gallic leaders told him that Hannibal had already crossed the Pyrenees. Scipio was shocked. He sent several hundred of his own cavalry galloping north with orders to find the army of Carthage.

As Hannibal's men prepared to continue toward the Alps, part of the Numidian scouting party thundered back into camp. They breathlessly described being surprised by Scipio's cavalry. A bloody battle had left 200 Numidians dead. The Romans had pursued the survivors to Carthage's camp before turning back.

Hannibal was certain that the Romans would arrive in a few days. He considered preparing a trap. But he could not afford to wait. It would soon be snowing in the Alps. He gave the order to pack up.

When the Romans arrived several days later, they found the Carthaginian campfires long cold.

# CHAPTER 7

# Over the Alps

FIERCE RESISTANCE AND
FROSTBITE make the final leg of
the journey the hardest yet.

AFTER TWO MORE WEEKS OF MARCHING,
the exhausted army of Carthage reached the looming
Alps—only to find another obstacle in their way.
They had entered the land of the fierce and powerful
Allobroges Celts. Hannibal's scouts found an
Allobroges army patrolling the rocky slopes above
the trail into the mountains.

Hannibal sent the scouts back to spy on the
Allobroges. The spies returned to report that the

HANNIBAL PREPARED to do what no general had ever
done before. He would take thousands of soldiers, as well as
horses and elephants, over the Alps.

Allobroges guarded the trail only during daylight. Each night they went home to their villages.

Hannibal saw his chance. To convince the Allobroges that he had settled in for the night, Hannibal ordered his army to set up camp and build cooking fires. After dark, he led a few thousand men up to the positions abandoned by the Allobroges.

At dawn, the rest of the army formed a column and began climbing the narrow trail, which overlooked a deep gorge. Seeing the Carthaginians on the move, the Allobroges sounded an alarm and scrambled for their posts. When they found Hannibal and his men already occupying the high ground, the stunned Celts hesitated. They looked up at Carthage's soldiers, then down at the long column of men and pack animals. Before Hannibal could attack, the Allobroges began rolling boulders and hurling rocks at the column below. Chaos broke out as terrified soldiers and beasts scrambled to escape the avalanche. Many fell into the gorge or were crushed by rocks.

THE ALLOBROGES CELTIC WARRIORS prepare to roll
boulders onto Carthaginian soldiers on the trail below.

Before his men suffered crippling losses, Hannibal
led a charge from above and scattered the Allobroges.

The Carthaginian army had been weakened but not
broken. They camped in the Allobroges villages for
three days and feasted on grain and beef. Before setting

out again they seized horses to replace the ones the Allobroges had killed.

The army now climbed higher and higher into the mountains. Winter was coming on fast, and the mountain air turned frigid. The men gasped for air as they trudged higher. Hunger gnawed at their bellies. Food had to be carefully rationed to make sure it lasted until they reached Italy. Every day, men and animals plunged thousands of feet to their deaths. Even more died from illness and the brutal cold. Exhausted soldiers slid off the trail and froze to death where they lay.

After more than ten days of climbing on frostbitten feet, the army at last reached the summit of the Alps. Hannibal stopped to rest his sick and tired men. A blizzard battered the camp with fierce winds and snow.

Sensing that his men were on the edge of despair, Hannibal knew he needed to do something. After the deadly blizzard passed, he brought his soldiers forward to a peak that overlooked lush green fields of the Po Valley. Hannibal gathered his strength and thundered:

IN THE HIGHEST PEAKS OF THE ALPS, treacherous
paths and freezing cold killed most of Hannibal's troops and
half of his elephants. His exhausted men were close to
quitting their mission to destroy Rome.

SPOTTING THE PO VALLEY in Italy, Hannibal assured his men
that their difficult journey was nearly over. The general promised they
would soon seize wealth and glory from their rich Roman enemies.

"You are now crossing the barriers not only of Italy, but of Rome itself. Henceforth all will be smooth and easy for you. In one or, at the most, two battles, you will be masters of the capital and stronghold of Italy."

As the men gazed at the valley, imagining the fresh loot and supplies to be found there, they began to cheer. Word spread through the ranks that the end of their journey was just a few days' march away.

After a five-day descent, the army of Carthage finally camped in the green valley. They had traveled five months from New Carthage to Italy. The losses were enormous. Only 20,000 infantry and 6,000 cavalry remained. Half the elephants were dead. Hannibal's army was much smaller, but its ranks held some of the strongest, most loyal soldiers a general ever commanded.

# Hannibal in Pictures

### SON OF CARTHAGE
In 247 B.C., Hannibal was born in Carthage, the center of the mighty Punic Empire.

### LIKE FATHER, LIKE SON
Hannibal's father, Hamilcar Barca, was a great Carthaginian general. He spent his life at war with the Romans, struggling for control of the Mediterranean Sea.

### CARTHAGE HUMILIATED
When Hannibal was six, the Roman Republic destroyed the Carthaginian navy, ending the First Punic War.

## ENEMY OF ROME FOREVER

Hamilcar asked his son to promise to hate Rome forever—and Hannibal agreed. Hamilcar then left for Iberia to set up a base from which he could attack Rome.

## TAKING COMMAND

Hannibal took control of the army of New Carthage after his father and brother-in-law were killed.

## BROKEN TREATY

New Carthage had signed a treaty promising to spare Saguntum, an Iberian city allied with Rome. But Hannibal attacked the city and slaughtered its inhabitants.

## HANNIBAL'S LIVING TANKS

The Carthaginians used war elephants to smash enemy formations. Hannibal took dozens of the elephants to Italy, but many died along the way.

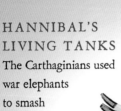

## A KILLER JOURNEY

The only way to invade Italy by land was through the Alps—icy and steep mountains full of fierce warriors. The Romans were shocked when Hannibal's army survived the passage.

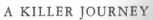

## FIRST BLOOD

The Romans suffered their first defeat by Hannibal near the banks of the Ticinus River. The Roman cavalry was no match for the fierce Numidians.

## A CLEVER TRICK

Surrounded by Romans, Hannibal ordered his men to tie torches to their pack animals to make it seem as though they were retreating. When the Romans chased the lights, Hannibal's army escaped.

## ROME'S NIGHTMARE
After Hannibal's forces killed 50,000 Roman soldiers at Cannae, the Carthaginians looted the bodies of their enemies.

## THE TIDE TURNS
A messenger presents Hannibal with his brother's head. Hasdrubal had stumbled into Roman armies while trying to bring more troops to Hannibal.

## TWO GREAT SOLDIERS MEET
The younger Scipio and Hannibal meet on the plain of Zama. Scipio had studied and learned from Hannibal's strategies.

## FINAL DISGRACE

During the Battle of Zama, Hannibal's elephants went berserk and trampled his cavalry. Hannibal's unprotected infantry was then wiped out.

## SCIPIO AFRICANUS

The younger Scipio was renamed Scipio Africanus in honor of his victory in North Africa. Here the great general is shown parading triumphantly through Rome.

## HANNIBAL'S END

Cornered by Roman troops, Hannibal drank poison and died. But his fearsome reputation lived on.

*Consider these questions as you read about how Hannibal inched farther and farther toward the heart of the Roman Empire.*

**BIG QUESTION:**

What were the strategies that Hannibal employed to outmaneuver the Roman army?

**RELATED QUESTIONS:**

- How did Hannibal use Sempronius's weakness to his advantage?

- What did Hannibal do to discover the local tribes' loyalties?

- How did Hannibal trap the Romans at Lake Trasimene?

- How did Hannibal outsmart and ultimately humiliate Flaminius?

# PART 3

Hannibal at the Gates

# CHAPTER 8

# "Conquer or Die"

Hannibal stages some gruesome
entertainment for his men and then
LEADS THEM INTO BATTLE.

HANNIBAL, IT SEEMED, HAD ACHIEVED
the impossible. But the toughest task still lay ahead:
Facing the great Roman legions—4,200-strong
divisions of armored infantry armed with javelins and
short stabbing swords.

Before meeting the Romans on the battlefield,
Hannibal needed food and reinforcements for his
26,000 starving men and animals. He approached a
tribe of local Gauls, the Taurinis, and encouraged them

to rise up against the Romans and join the army of Carthage. The Taurini chieftains refused. They were too busy fighting neighboring tribes.

Angry and in need of supplies, Hannibal decided to make an example of the Taurinis. His men surrounded their hilltop village. After a three-day siege, they stormed up the hill and massacred everyone they could find. Hannibal surveyed the town's smoldering ruins while his army devoured the food the Taurinis had stored for winter.

While the men rested, Hannibal's scouts brought news of the Roman army led by Scipio. The Romans had learned of the Carthaginians' arrival. Scipio was closing in fast, eager to catch the invaders before they regained their strength.

To inspire his soldiers for the coming battle, Hannibal provided them with a bloody spectacle. Prisoners seized during fighting in the Alps were brought before the army in chains. Hannibal asked the prisoners which of them would be willing to fight a fellow prisoner to the death. The victor, he explained, would win his freedom and a horse.

All the prisoners begged for the chance to fight. Several pairs chosen by lottery fought before the assembled army. The soldiers enjoyed the blood sport. As promised, the survivors were released.

Now Hannibal addressed his men. "Soldiers, you have seen in the fate of others an example of how to conquer or die," he said. The men roared their approval.

Hannibal went on to explain that the men were in the same situation as the prisoners. Italy was surrounded by water and mountains; they had no escape route. "On this spot where you will for the first time encounter the enemy, you must either conquer or die."

The men roared again, anxious for a chance to fight. In a matter of days, they got their wish.

Hannibal found Scipio's army camped near the Ticinus River. He moved the army of Carthage into position on the other side of the water. The Romans built a temporary bridge and crossed it to an open field. Hannibal watched them come, their helmets and breastplates gleaming, marching in perfect formation. They were the best-trained, most-disciplined soldiers in the world. But Hannibal was confident. He lined his men up in standard battle formation—infantry in the center, cavalry to either side. At last, Hannibal would have his chance to spill Roman blood.

As was the custom, the battle began when the opposing cavalries raced onto the open ground and clashed. Soon, Hannibal's powerful Numidian horsemen broke through and scattered the Roman infantry. The horsemen chased down hundreds of Romans and slashed them to death as they fled. Hannibal's infantry surged forward to join the fight. But Scipio quickly pulled his troops back across the river and destroyed the bridge to prevent the Carthaginians from following.

Scipio was wounded during the retreat and would have been taken prisoner but for the aid of his 17-year-old son. The young soldier, also named Publius Scipio,

persuaded a group of Romans to race with him into the fighting and rescue his father.

It would not be the last time the younger Scipio led a charge against Hannibal's men.

In the end, the defeat was a minor one for Rome. Still, Hannibal had proven that he would not easily be beaten.

THE YOUNGER SCIPIO DEFENDS his wounded father on the banks of the Ticinus River. This would be the first of Hannibal's many victories against the hated Romans.

The Romans retreated to a heavily fortified camp near the Trebia River. Hannibal led his army eastward along the Po River in pursuit. When he found the Romans, he boldly demanded that the elder Scipio leave his fortified camp and come to the battlefield for a full-scale fight on level ground. Perhaps there, Hannibal would get his first true taste of victory.

# ROME'S LEGIONS

HANNIBAL HAD TO RELY ON MERCENARIES —foreign soldiers who fought for money. But the Romans had a highly disciplined standing army—a professional force that trained in times of peace as well as war. Most Roman men could be called to serve as needed for 20 years. They were led by commanders called consuls. A Roman assembly of military leaders elected two consuls to head the government. In times of war, consuls also commanded the army.

Consuls depended on the discipline and skill of their foot soldiers rather than the speed of their cavalry. Cavalry troops were generally aristocrats who could afford horses. Roman commanders scrambled to improve their cavalry after Hannibal's Numidians dominated early battles in the Second Punic War.

A ROMAN CITIZEN-SOLDIER

# CHAPTER 9

# Battle of Trebia

An over-eager Roman consul plays
RIGHT INTO HANNIBAL'S HANDS.

CAMPED ON THE BANKS OF THE TREBIA
River, Scipio ignored Hannibal's call for a fight. He
was determined to give himself and his men a rest.

It wasn't long before a group of Scipio's Gallic
soldiers disturbed his plan. The Gauls took notice of
Hannibal's strength and decided they would be better
off fighting for Carthage. One night, they murdered a
group of sleeping Roman soldiers and decapitated the
corpses. They raced into Hannibal's camp carrying the
Roman heads as gruesome proof that they were not spies.

Hannibal ordered the Gauls to return to their villages and recruit fellow tribesmen who were ready to rise up against their Roman rulers.

The desertion of the Gauls left Scipio in a dangerous position. He could no longer trust the loyalty of the local tribes. Fearing an attack, the Roman Senate sent its second consul, Sempronius, and his army to aid Scipio.

As required by Roman law, Scipio and Sempronius alternated command of the combined armies. Scipio led the forces one day, Sempronius the next. Scipio was a cautious man, reluctant to fight unless he had a clear advantage. Sempronius, by contrast, was impatient, eager for a victory to increase his prestige in Rome.

Knowing his enemy, Hannibal decided to lure Sempronius into battle. Hannibal's camp looked across a wide field perfect for Carthage's cavalry. And thick bushes nearby could hide a small army. Hannibal placed his brother Mago and several thousand of his best soldiers in the bushes. He would lure the Romans onto the chosen battlefield and then spring an ambush.

On a morning of Sempronius's command, Hannibal saw to it that his soldiers awoke early and ate a good breakfast. It was a cold day in late December 218 B.C.. His men warmed themselves before roaring fires and rubbed their limbs with heated oil. They were ready to fight.

Hannibal then sent 1,000 cavalry toward the enemy camp. Roman bugles blared an alarm. Just as Hannibal had hoped, Sempronius ordered his sleepy army into battle.

The two sides met on the field Hannibal had chosen. Carthage's 28,000 infantry and 10,000 cavalry faced 36,000 Roman infantry and 4,000 cavalry. Cold, tired, and hungry, the Romans launched a frontal assault. The hand-to-hand combat was brutal and bloody. Neither force could gain an advantage.

Hannibal broke the stalemate by sending his cavalry into battle with a line of elephants thundering in front. The Romans were terrified. Many of them had never seen an elephant before. The Roman cavalry panicked and fled. Hannibal's elephants and horsemen then wheeled around and attacked the exposed Roman infantry. At the same time, Mago sprang his ambush. A storm of spears and rocks hit the Romans from behind as Mago's men burst from their hiding places and plunged into the fight.

Surrounded, the legions fought bravely. About 10,000 Romans managed to hack through the Carthaginian line and make their way to a nearby village. The rest grew too weary to fight. Many of them were trampled by the elephants. By the time the fighting ended, one-third of Sempronius's force had been killed.

In little more than a month, Hannibal had swept down from the Alps and torn apart the best of the Roman legions. At the Ticinus River, Scipio had gotten a small taste of the general's military genius. Now, Sempronius had felt the full power of the battle-hardened army of Carthage, complete with the fearsome Numidian cavalry and gigantic thundering elephants. It must have seemed as though Hannibal had come to Italy not out of the mountains, but from another world.

C H A P T E R  1 0

# Ambush!

## HANNIBAL LAYS A TRAP
## at Lake Trasimene.

HANNIBAL SPENT THE WINTER ROAMING
through northern Italy. He raided villages for
supplies and rested his men while his enemy
retreated to winter quarters. There would be little
fighting until spring. During the lull, Hannibal is
said to have disguised himself and moved among the
local tribes to learn whether they were loyal to him.
In the spring, Hannibal rallied his troops and headed
south toward his ultimate goal: the city of Rome.

Between Hannibal and Rome stood the Apennine Mountains. Hoping to move quickly into the rich farmland of Etruria just south of the mountains, Hannibal chose the most direct route possible. The trip went well until the army arrived at the soggy marshland surrounding the Arno River. With each step, the terrible muck sucked at the legs of the soldiers and horses. For three days, the men had only one place to rest—on top of mules that had died of exhaustion. Hannibal contracted a painful infection in his eyes. In agony, he had to be carried atop the only elephant that had survived the winter. He ultimately lost sight in one eye.

The trip was costly but effective. Hannibal was just a few hundred miles north of Rome, with villages to plunder. He went on the march again with a Roman army in close pursuit. Hannibal burned villages and fields, all the while looking for a place to set a trap for the Romans. In June, with the Roman army a day's march behind him, Hannibal found what he had been looking for. He reined in his horse and ordered his army to halt. An open field large enough for a massive battle lay before him. The field was bordered on the right by Lake Trasimene and on the left by a wide ring of hills. Surveying the terrain, Hannibal imagined not simply victory, but complete destruction of the Roman legions.

Hannibal set up a highly visible camp at the far end of the field. The Romans soon arrived and camped at the other end, between the lake and the hills. The

WHILE STRUGGLING THROUGH the marshes surrounding the Arno River, Hannibal developed a terrible eye infection that later cost him his vision in one eye. The injury did not appear to slow him down.

legions were led by a newly elected consul named Flaminius, and he was anxious for battle. Little did he know that he was stepping right into Hannibal's trap.

After dark, Hannibal set up his plan. He secretly moved most of his soldiers behind the hills, leaving his tents where the Romans could see them. He posted the deadly Numidian cavalry at a narrow passage between the lake and the hills, cutting off the only exit from the battlefield.

In the morning, the Roman bugles sounded. Mists rising from the lake made it difficult to see. Flaminius assembled his legions. They lined up to attack the Carthaginian camp, which was still visible at the end of the field. Hannibal sent the soldiers he had left at the camp forward to wait for the Romans on flat ground. His hidden infantry and cavalry waited silently in the foggy hills as the Romans marched below them.

The Roman bugles sounded again. Roaring their battle cry, the legions surged forward. They hurled their javelins into Hannibal's front line and charged. Now

Hannibal launched his ambush. From the hills to the left of the Romans came a barrage of javelins and rocks followed by thousands of soldiers. Then the terrified Romans heard thousands of pounding hooves as the swift Numidians crashed into them from behind.

Flaminius's men did not stand a chance. Trapped on one side by the lake and the other three by Hannibal's army, they fought desperately to escape. Flaminius galloped bravely amid the chaotic fighting. Wearing the flamboyant armor and helmet of a commander, he made an obvious target. He was spotted by a Gallic horseman whose village had been destroyed by Flaminius. The Gaul charged forward and killed Flaminius's bodyguard. Then he plunged his spear into the consul.

Near the end of the fighting, many of the Romans tried to escape into the lake. Dressed in their heavy armor, some drowned. Others stood helplessly in water up to their chins. The Numidian cavalry galloped in after them. Splashing and shouting, they cut down the helpless Romans one by one.

HANNIBAL'S TROOPS HACK at helpless Romans after the
ambush at Lake Trasimene. Flaminius, the outwitted Roman
commander, was killed along with 15,000 of his men.

The Roman troops who had marched at the front of the column escaped destruction for a time. Seeing the hopeless slaughter behind them, they fled to the next village. They were later surrounded and captured. Hannibal had the Romans put in chains and fed only enough to keep them alive. Non-Romans were sent home to their villages to tell of what they had seen and hopefully bring new recruits to the army of Carthage.

The Roman legions had never before suffered such a devastating defeat. An estimated 15,000 Romans died and as many were taken prisoner. The Carthaginians collected enough armor and helmets from the Roman dead to equip the entire Libyan infantry.

Reports of the terrible defeat at Lake Trasimene made it to Rome within days. For the second time, the Romans had met Hannibal on ground he had chosen and ended up surrounded and defeated. The mighty Roman legions seemed no match for the invader, who was now just a week's march from Rome. The city erupted in panic. How could Hannibal be stopped?

# CHAPTER 11

# The Delayer

## A new Roman commander tries to WEAR HANNIBAL DOWN.

AFTER THE BLOODBATH AT LAKE Trasimene, Hannibal was in position to march on Rome. But the city was still well defended. He doubted he had the manpower to seize it. Instead, he hoped that his success on the battlefield would make the Romans beg for peace. So Hannibal simply marched through central Italy, burning and pillaging villages and farmland along the way.

The Romans, meanwhile, took steps to strengthen their defenses. They named Quintus Fabius Maximus as dictator—an emergency position with unlimited power. Under his direction, the army drafted more soldiers and fortified the walls of the city. A force was sent to Iberia to press the war against Hasdrubal. Meanwhile, the navy made sure that neither Hasdrubal nor Carthage could send supplies or reinforcements to Hannibal in Italy.

Fabius also decided to change tactics against the invaders. Carthage's vastly superior cavalry put Roman forces at a terrible disadvantage on open ground. On the

KNOWING THAT THE REPUBLIC was in mortal danger, the Roman government took a drastic step and declared Fabius its dictator. It was hoped that Fabius would use his powers to crush Hannibal, but the new dictator chose to delay and harass instead.

other hand, Rome had more soldiers than Hannibal and better access to supplies. Hannibal's army needed to loot farms and villages to survive.

Fabius's new plan was to avoid an all-out battle with Hannibal. Instead, Roman forces would block the Carthaginian from moving easily and limit his access to food and supplies until his army was worn out. Once Hannibal was weakened, the Roman legions would move in for the kill.

For the rest of the year, Fabius and Hannibal played a game of cat and mouse. Fabius stayed close enough to annoy the army of Carthage. Roman cavalry attacked any small groups of soldiers sent out to gather supplies. But the Roman infantry stayed on high ground where Carthaginian horsemen couldn't reach them.

Hannibal kept moving south through Italy, destroying villages as he went. He hoped to provoke Fabius into an attack. But the Roman soldiers merely stood and watched as smoke rose from the farms and villages around them. Hannibal picked up some new recruits as he traveled, but most villagers considered the Carthaginian to be a cruel invader rather than a liberator. He failed to ignite the massive rebellion he was hoping for.

At the end of the summer, Hannibal led his men to the fertile plains of Campania, 150 miles south of Rome. For weeks, he destroyed fields and villages there. Still Fabius refused to fight. As the cold weather descended, Hannibal decided his men needed to find winter quarters farther from Rome, where they could safely wait for spring.

Hannibal's plan was to go through the mountains to the east of Campania. But when he arrived at the mountain pass, 4,000 of Fabius's men stood guard. The rest of the Roman army lay camped on a hill nearby. To fight the Romans from below would be foolish. It looked as though the army of Carthage was trapped.

But once again, Hannibal devised a strategy. The Carthaginians set up camp below the Romans. They ate an early dinner and prepared to march through the night. When darkness fell, the army's many oxen and cattle were brought forward and torches were tied to their horns. The animal keepers lit the torches and led their cattle into the hills surrounding the pass.

The Roman sentries immediately sounded an alarm, thinking that hundreds of men with torches were

FABIUS THOUGHT HE HAD trapped Hannibal. But the wily Carthaginian ordered his men to tie torches to the pack animals and send them away. That way, the Romans would think the soldiers were retreating. When the Romans chased the lights, Hannibal's men escaped into the mountains.

moving up the hillsides. Thousands of Roman soldiers hurried to meet the torch-bearing army. Meanwhile, Hannibal's men marched quietly through the unguarded pass. When the Romans realized what had happened it was too late. The darkness made it impossible to launch an effective attack.

Fabius was humiliated. For the better part of a year, the mighty Roman legions had stood by while an invader destroyed their land. Soldiers were getting restless. Village leaders were demanding protection from Hannibal. Tired of their leader's tactics, Romans began calling Fabius "The Delayer."

Finally, the senators decided to act. When Fabius's term ended, the Senate nominated a pair of more aggressive consuls, Varro and Paullus. The new consuls were given the power to create the biggest army ever deployed. Their job: Destroy Hannibal and his invading force as soon as possible.

Now Hannibal would get the fight he wanted.

CHAPTER 12

# Battle of Cannae

## The Romans suffer
## ANOTHER TERRIBLE DEFEAT.

IN THE SPRING OF 216 B.C., HANNIBAL brought the army of Carthage out of winter quarters and issued a challenge to the new Roman consuls. He seized Cannae, a village on the southeastern coast of Italy. Cannae was a major supply depot for the Romans, and the Roman consuls wanted it back. Scouts soon told Hannibal that an enormous Roman force—at least 80,000 infantry and 6,000 cavalry—had marched within six miles. Hannibal had only 40,000 infantry and 10,000 cavalry to oppose them.

The two armies faced off in a field near Cannae for what leaders on both sides hoped would be the decisive battle of the war. Hannibal, as always, was ready with a plan. He placed his weakest infantry at the center of his line, and then personally led them forward so that the line curved outward toward the Romans. He placed the stronger Libyans to either side of this bulge. The Numidians lined up to the right, where open ground would give them room to maneuver their horses. The rest of the cavalry lined up to the left.

Varro, the Roman consul in command that day, planned to crush the heart of Hannibal's army. He aimed the bulk of his enormous force at the center of Carthage's line. Row upon row of soldiers waited for the order to charge. The noise was terrible as each infantry howled at the other, banging their shields and stomping.

Finally, Hannibal's cavalry let out a yell and charged the Roman horsemen in a cloud of dust. It didn't take long for the Numidians to destroy the Roman cavalry.

But as soon as the Roman horsemen were off the field, the mighty legions began their attack. The Romans flung their javelins as they advanced. Hannibal's Balearic slingers returned a shower of rocks and lead. Slowly, the Roman infantry forced the Carthaginian center backwards until the bulge had been erased. The Romans surged forward, forcing their enemy to give ground—just as Hannibal had planned.

Hannibal's Libyan infantry stood away from the main fighting and watched the Romans move into their general's trap. The Roman soldiers had unknowingly pushed forward into the center of a pincer—a giant U shape formed by Libyans to either side of them and Hannibal's retreating center line in front.

At a signal from Hannibal, the Libyans at last let out a battle cry and slammed into the flanks of the massive Roman force. The Romans found themselves so close together that they could not effectively turn and resist. The Libyans took full advantage, slashing their way into the enemy fighters. Hannibal galloped back and forth on his horse, urging his men to fight and kill. His plan was working to perfection.

Meanwhile, the bulk of Carthage's cavalry raced in and attacked the desperate Romans from behind. Completely surrounded, the Romans fought bravely as always. But the legions were being slowly ground up by the swarming Carthaginians.

The slaughter must have horrified even Hannibal. The chests of his warhorses and the shields of his infantry grew slick with Roman blood. The Libyans, Gauls, and Iberians had to stop now and again to rest from the merciless slaughter. They hacked at the Romans until their swords grew dull from overuse. Whenever a Roman soldier managed to drag himself from a pile of bodies, he was quickly cut down.

By the end of the day, 50,000 Romans had perished at Cannae.

When the bloodshed was over, Hannibal and his commanders met to plan their next move. They had just destroyed one of the largest armies ever to take the

AFTER THE VICTORY at Cannae, Hannibal's brother
Mago returned to Carthage and presented the Senate with
a treasure: the rings of killed Romans.

field. Would there ever be a better time to march on Rome? Maharbal, commander of the Numidian cavalry, urged Hannibal to seize the moment and finish the war. "I prophesy that in five days you will be feasting as victor in [Rome]," he insisted.

On the verge of total victory, Hannibal could not bring himself to give the command. He praised Maharbal for his bold spirit. Then the great general told him that the time had not yet come to lay siege to Rome.

Maharbal was disappointed and disillusioned, and he let his commander know how he felt. "The gods have not given all their gifts to one man," he said. "You know how to win victory, Hannibal; you do not how to use it."

# War of Attrition

## The fight for Italy
## DRAGS ON, AND ON, AND ON.

INSTEAD OF MARCHING ON ROME, Hannibal settled into a long stalemate with the Romans. The army of Carthage continued to plunder southern Italy, and over the next few years, they seemed to gain momentum. Shortly after the Battle of Cannae, the city of Capua defected from the Roman Republic and joined Carthage. Capua's support gave Hannibal a base about 100 miles southeast of Rome. In 212 B.C., Hannibal seized the city of Tarentum, near the southeastern tip of Italy. His

HANNIBAL'S TROOPS STORM the city of Tarentum. Huge
numbers of Roman soldiers died during this battle, and once again
it seemed that their republic was in mortal danger.

men killed two Roman consuls and destroyed their armies. Once again, it seemed like he might achieve the impossible.

But soon, the tide began to turn. The Romans surrounded Capua, Hannibal's stronghold. Again and again, Hannibal's men attacked the Roman lines, trying to break through and relieve the city. Each time they were turned back with heavy losses.

Finally, Hannibal put a desperate plan into action. He hurried north toward Rome with a large group of soldiers, hoping to draw the Roman armies away from Capua.

For several days in 211 B.C., Hannibal and his army camped outside the walls of Rome. The city closed its gates and readied for attack. But Hannibal had no intention of launching an assault. He waited for the Roman armies to arrive and fight. But they refused to take the bait. They remained at Capua, and before long, the city fell to the Romans.

Legend has it that one moonless night, while camped near Rome, Hannibal rode to within a few yards of the city walls. Supposedly, he climbed down from his horse and flung his javelin with all his strength towards the city. The weapon sailed over the wall and clattered into the street below.

This empty gesture would be mighty Hannibal's only direct assault on Rome.

For the next few years, Hannibal trudged on. But his glory days in Italy were over. Cut off from his homeland, he barely kept his army alive in a hostile land with the most feared fighting force in the world in pursuit.

The news from the rest of the Punic Empire was equally bad. The younger Publius Scipio, who had saved his father's life at the battle of Ticinus, had taken over Roman forces in Iberia. A well-educated man, Scipio carefully studied the tactics of Hannibal and used them to great effect. In 208 B.C., he defeated the army of Hannibal's brother Hasdrubal at Baecula, in central Iberia.

Hasdrubal hurried his remaining soldiers over the Alps and into Italy. But before he could rejoin

HANNIBAL RECOILS AT A GIFT from Nero—his brother
Hasdrubal's severed head. The loss of Hasdrubal and his troops was
devastating for Hannibal—there was no one to reinforce his army.

Hannibal, he was attacked by Roman armies at the Metaurus River, in northern Italy. Outnumbered, Hasdrubal and most of his troops were killed. Roman consul Claudius Nero ordered his head cut off and flung into Hannibal's camp.

After crushing the remaining Carthaginian armies in Iberia, Scipio decided to strike at the heart of the Punic Empire. In 204 B.C., he landed 35,000 men on the shores of North Africa and began carving his way through the Kingdom of Numidia toward Carthage. The following year, the Carthaginian Senate sent a message to Hannibal in Italy: He was needed desperately in Africa.

For 15 years, Hannibal had outwitted and outfought the most powerful nation in the world. But for one day of indecision, he might have seized Rome and toppled the Roman Republic. Now, he was returning home for a last attempt to save his homeland from destruction.

*Consider these questions as you read about Hannibal's final years.*

**BIG QUESTION:**

How did Hannibal's crusade against the Romans finally end?

**RELATED QUESTIONS:**

- What strategies did Scipio use to gain advantage at the Battle of Zama?

- What were the terms of the peace treaty that finally ended the Second Punic War?

🏛

# PART 4

# Final

# Years

# CHAPTER 14

# The Meeting

## Hannibal and Scipio
### MEET AT LAST.

HANNIBAL REACHED AFRICA IN 203 B.C. with the haggard remains of his army. Scipio's legions were closing in on Carthage, and the pro-war party in the Carthaginian Senate was eager to fight back. They added local recruits to Hannibal's veterans and asked Hannibal to attack Scipio's army immediately. But Hannibal rested his men on the plains outside of Carthage and waited. As always, he was looking for the moment that would give him the greatest advantage.

Hannibal sent a group of scouts to assess the enemy's strength. When three of these spies were captured and brought before Scipio, the Roman commander ordered that they be given a full tour of the Roman forces. They were then sent back to report to Hannibal on all they had seen. Hannibal was fascinated by Scipio's boldness. Here was an enemy who no doubt reminded Hannibal of himself.

Finally, in October 202 B.C., Hannibal moved his army to a hillside within four miles of Scipio's camp. He sent messengers to arrange a meeting with Scipio. The next morning, Hannibal and his bodyguard rode out to the plain of Zama. Scipio and his guard galloped towards them. Soon, each commander left his bodyguard behind. They walked together, with only an interpreter between them.

The generals were similar in many ways: intelligent, well-educated noblemen and brilliant strategists. Livy wrote of the incredible meeting: "They were not only the two greatest soldiers of their time, but the

SCIPIO AND HANNIBAL MEET at the plain of Zama.
Knowing his army was overmatched, Hannibal asked for peace. But
Scipio was determined to crush Carthage once and for all.

equals of any king or commander in the whole history
of the world."

Hannibal, his face weathered from years of struggle,
spoke to his younger enemy with respect. He asked for
peace, telling Scipio, "It would have been far better had
the gods [made Rome] . . . satisfied with sovereignty of
Italy, while we were contented with Africa."

Hannibal advised Scipio to take Iberia and the rest
of the non-African territory he had conquered and stop

fighting. Carthage, he promised, would never again attempt to expand beyond Africa. "Do not expose so many years' good fortune to the hazard of a single hour [of battle]," he advised.

For Scipio, it was no doubt awe-inspiring to meet the commander who had nearly destroyed the Roman Republic. But the Roman general was not convinced. "Had you of your own free will left Italy . . . before I sailed for Africa and then come with proposals for peace, I admit that I would have acted too proudly and unfairly had I rejected them," Scipio said. But now, the Roman continued, it was too late for peace. Carthage must surrender unconditionally or fight.

Hannibal and Scipio rode back to their camps and prepared their men for battle.

CHAPTER 15

# Battle of Zama

## HANNIBAL MAKES HIS
## LAST STAND against the Romans.

THE MORNING AFTER THE MEETING between Hannibal and Scipio, the two armies lined up for battle. Both forces numbered about 40,000 men. For once, Hannibal had fewer cavalry than the Romans, who had allied with thousands of Numidian horsemen during their rampage through North Africa.

Hannibal split his troops into three horizontal lines with his best veteran infantry in the rear. Cavalry stood to either side of the infantry. In front of them all towered 80 elephants poised to charge through Roman lines.

Hannibal wanted the elephants and the first two lines of infantry to soften the Roman legions. Then his veterans in the third line would join the fight and finish it.

Scipio matched this arrangement—with one important difference. He left regularly spaced open lanes among his men. The elephants had been trained to run in a straight line, and Scipio hoped they might rumble harmlessly through the gaps.

At Hannibal's signal, the elephants took off, pounding toward the Romans. The Battle of Zama had begun. The Romans sounded their bugles and beat their swords against their shields. The noise sent the elephant herd into a frenzy. Some turned and ran back into Hannibal's lines. Their size and smell spooked the Carthaginian horses, which reared and balked. Seeing the disorder, the Roman cavalry charged and chased Hannibal's horsemen into retreat.

Meanwhile, the rest of the elephants had thundered into the Roman lines. Some raced harmlessly through the open lanes. But many—even as they were pelted

HANNIBAL HOPED his elephants could crush the Roman lines, but Scipio had a plan. His men used bugles to frighten the beasts. They plunged back into Hannibal's army and scattered his cavalry.

with spears and rocks—crashed into the infantry. Hundreds of Romans were gored or trampled.

His cavalry on the defensive, Hannibal was faced with an unusual situation: Success lay in the hands of the Carthaginian infantry. With raging battle cries, Hannibal's front lines charged to meet Scipio's legions. For hours, men fought and died. At times, the piles of dead bodies made it difficult to fight. At one point, Scipio's buglers sounded a recall. The wounded were carried to the rear and the armies reorganized.

When they charged again, the noise and suffering grew. Hannibal at last hurled his best infantry into the fight. He believed they would break the tiring Roman line and deliver victory. If they failed, all was lost for Carthage.

Now, in a twist of fate, the cavalry turned the battle against Hannibal. Having finished off Carthage's cavalry, Scipio's horsemen returned to the field. They relentlessly attacked the flanks and rear of Hannibal's infantry. Like the Roman consuls at Trasimene and Cannae, Hannibal watched helplessly as his army fell into chaos. Completely surrounded, thousands of Hannibal's men were slaughtered. When the battle ended, 20,000 lay dead. Another 20,000 were prisoners of the Romans.

Exhausted and unable to do anything more to save his men, Hannibal escaped to Carthage with a few cavalry. At age 45, his days as commander of a mighty army had ended.

# CHAPTER 16

# Final Defeat

## Hannibal swallows his pride and MAKES PEACE WITH HIS ENEMY.

AFTER THE DISASTER ON THE PLAIN OF Zama, Carthage sent envoys to Scipio seeking peace. Scipio, who won the title Scipio Africanus for his victory in Africa, sent the envoys back with harsh terms. Carthage was to give up Iberia, pay a fortune to Rome, dismantle what was left of its army, and destroy all but ten ships in its naval fleet.

A great debate followed in the Carthaginian Senate. Hannibal, who had won his reputation as a war hero in

SCIPIO, NAMED SCIPIO AFRICANUS in honor of his victory in North Africa, is carried triumphantly into Rome. The Roman general showed little mercy for Carthage, but Hannibal knew his people had to accept Scipio's harsh terms.

some of the most daring battles in history, now stood for peace. When a senator rose to insist that Carthage reject Scipio's terms, Hannibal strode to the podium and dragged the man to his seat. Standing in the senator's place, Hannibal pointed out that the terms could have been worse. Had the Romans laid siege to Carthage, he said, the result would have been terrible suffering. "So now I beg you," he told the senators. "Do not even discuss the matter but agree unanimously to the proposal for peace."

The senators reluctantly agreed. The peace treaty was signed, finally bringing an end to the Second Punic War. Hannibal soon looked on as hundreds of Carthage's ships were towed to sea and burned. As agreed, Hannibal handed over his battle elephants and prisoners of war. He returned Rome's escaped slaves and deserters. Scipio saved the worst punishment for his deserters. Non-Romans were beheaded and the Roman citizens were crucified.

The year was 201 B.C. For 17 years, Hannibal had devoted himself to the destruction of Rome. He and his army had conquered Iberia, crossed the Alps, and destroyed entire Roman armies on the hills and plains of Italy.

Now, all was lost. Rome ruled Iberia, most of North Africa, and the Mediterranean Sea. Carthage itself was little more than a Roman colony. Far from bringing about the end of Rome, Hannibal had seen the republic rise to become the mightiest nation ever known.

# CHAPTER 17

# A Lonely End

## Hannibal ends his days as
## A REFUGEE FROM HIS OWN LAND.

AT AGE 45, HANNIBAL ENTERED THE LAST phase of his eventful life. For some years, he remained in command of what was left of Carthage's army. It is said he put them to work farming in the ruined countryside.

Many Roman officials, convinced that Hannibal was still plotting against Rome, wanted him arrested. Interestingly, Scipio told the Roman Senate that to persecute a man of Hannibal's stature was beneath the dignity of the republic.

Despite Hannibal's defeat, ordinary Carthaginians revered the famous general. Hannibal used his influence to win election to Carthage's Senate, where he fought corruption. In the process, he made many enemies. He hounded lawmakers who used their position to grow wealthy through bribes and other crimes. These men plotted to get rid of Hannibal. Others hated him for launching the war that brought the Romans to Africa. There were plenty of people in Carthage who would have been happy to see Hannibal carried off to Rome in chains.

Around 195 B.C., Hannibal fled from his enemies in Carthage. For years he moved from one king's court to another, always one step ahead of the Romans. While living in Bythinia, near present-day Istanbul, he fought as a navy admiral against Roman allies in Greece. Under his orders, clay jars filled with poisonous snakes were catapulted onto the opposing king's ship. This ingenious attack made Hannibal the first commander to use a biological weapon in warfare.

In 183 B.C., Roman soldiers finally caught up with Hannibal. They surrounded his house in Bythinia. The aging general drank poison rather than surrender. "Let us relieve the Romans from the anxiety they have so long experienced," Hannibal supposedly grumbled, "since they think it tries their patience too much to wait for an old man's death."

HANNIBAL DRINKS POISON, ending Rome's long nightmare. Now the Roman Republic was free to extend control over all the Mediterranean.

# *Wicked?*

About 40 years after Hannibal's death, Rome and Carthage went to war again, in the Third Punic War. The adopted grandson of Scipio Africanus led the victorious Roman army. When they finally triumphed, Roman forces erased all traces of the city. Its buildings and harbor were pounded to dust.

Carthage was no more, but Hannibal's memory still survived in Rome. For generations, Romans grew up hearing tales of the fearsome commander's cruelty. Roman housewives threatened to turn over misbehaving children to Hannibal for punishment. Long after his defeat, whenever the Roman Republic faced a crisis an agitated senator might shout: "Hannibal ad portus!" ("Hannibal is at the gates!"). This phrase is still used today.

But was Hannibal truly wicked? He was a military genius whose tactics are still studied more than 2,000 years after his death. Modern generals try to copy the pincer strategy he used to destroy the Romans at Cannae and his use of ambush to defeat large forces.

Certainly, Hannibal was involved in savage fighting. He used brutal tactics, and innocent people were murdered at his command. But he did not kill for pleasure. Various Roman generals used similar methods of terrorizing their enemies. The Romans even built statues in Hannibal's honor.

Winston Churchill, another famous wartime leader, once said, "History is written by the victors." In no case is this truer than in Hannibal's. No record of Carthage survives that was written by a Carthaginian. The most influential writer documenting the Second Punic War, Titus Livy (59 B.C.–A.D. 17), was a Roman. Livy viewed history as a series of moral lessons and almost surely exaggerated Hannibal's cruelty.

Had Hannibal and Carthage triumphed, the greatest enemy Rome ever faced might be remembered as the great African liberator of Italy, Spain, and France.

# READINGS FROM ANCIENT TIMES

When studying people and events of the past, historians seek firsthand evidence. They turn to primary sources, original documents or objects created during the time they are studying.

Few primary sources survive from ancient times. So historians also rely on secondary sources, created after actual events took place. Especially helpful are accounts by ancient historians, which often draw from original materials that are now lost.

Three such historians are the Greek writers Appian and Polybius and the Roman writer Titus Livius, known as Livy. Excerpts from their works on Hannibal follow. Polybius's history is particularly valuable because it is based on eyewitness accounts.

All sources, whether primary or secondary, must be examined for reliability and possible bias. Historians understand that such accounts provide different points of view about the same events. Taken together, they bring us to a fuller understanding of the past.

# FROM ROMAN HISTORY

*Writing in the second century, the Greek historian Appian
describes Hannibal's early career. According to Appian,
Hannibal exaggerates and lies to win support. He is not only
bloodthirsty in battle but also tricks the Gauls into believing
he is divine.*

Hannibal was chosen by the army as the third commander in Spain because he seemed to have great aptitude
and fondness for war.... Believing, as was the fact, that a
war between the Romans and Carthaginians once begun
would last a long time, and that the undertaking would
bring great glory to himself, even if he should fail (it
was said, also, that he had been sworn on the altar by his
father, while yet a boy, that he would be an eternal enemy
of Rome), he resolved to cross the Iberus in defiance of
the treaty.

For a pretext he procured certain persons to make accusations against the Saguntines. By continually forwarding

these accusations to Carthage, and by accusing the Romans of secretly inciting the Spaniards to revolt, he obtained permission from Carthage to take such steps as he should think fit. Thereupon he crossed the Iberus and destroyed the city of Saguntum with its inhabitants. Thus the treaty, made between the Romans and the Carthaginians after the war in Sicily, was broken....

...After a brief pause he attacked Taurasia, a Gallic town, took it by storm, and put the prisoners to death, in order to strike terror into the rest of the Gauls....

These exploits, one after another, following his passage of the Alps, exalted Hannibal's fame among the Cisalpine Gauls as an invincible commander and one most highly favored by fortune.

In order to increase the admiration of those barbarians, who were easily deceived, he frequently changed his clothes and his hair.... When the Gauls saw him moving among their people now an old man, then a young man, and again a middle-aged man, and continually changing from one to the other, they were astonished and thought that he partook of the divine nature....

*Source:* Appian, *Roman History,* trans. by Horace White, Loeb Classical Library (Cambridge: Harvard University Press, 1912).

# FROM THE HISTORY OF ROME

*In 25 B.C., the Roman historian Titus Livius, known as Livy, began writing his History of Rome—more than 100 years after Hannibal died. In this excerpt Livy describes Hannibal's character as a mixture of "virtue and vices"; he is brave, yet cruel.*

Hannibal, having been sent into Spain, from his very first arrival drew the eyes of the whole army upon him. The veteran soldiers imagined that Hamilcar (Hannibal's father), in his youth, was restored to them; they remarked the same vigor in his looks and animation in his eye the same features and expression of countenance....

...There never was a genius more fitted for the two most opposite duties of obeying and commanding; so that you could not easily decide whether he were dearer to the general or the army... His fearlessness in encountering dangers, and his prudence when in the midst of them, were extreme. His body could not be exhausted, nor his mind subdued, by any toil. He could alike endure either heat or cold. The quantity of his food and drink was determined by the wants of nature, and not by pleasure.... The time that remained after the transaction of business was given to repose; but that repose was neither invited by a soft bed nor by quiet.

Many have seen him wrapped in a military cloak, lying on the ground amid the watches and outposts of the soldiers. His dress was not at all superior to that of his equals: his arms and his horses were conspicuous. He was at once by far the first of the cavalry and infantry; and, foremost to advance to the charge, was last to leave the engagement.

Excessive vices counterbalanced these high virtues of the hero; inhuman cruelty, more than Punic perfidy, no truth, no reverence for things sacred, no fear of the gods, no respect for oaths, no sense of religion. With a character thus made up of virtue and vices, he served for three years under the command of Hasdrubal, without neglecting anything which ought to be done or seen by one who was to become a great general.

*Source:* Titus Livius, *The History of Rome,* trans. by D. Spillan (London: Henry G. Bohn, 1868).

# From The Histories

*Writing in the second century B.C., the Greek historian
Polybius re-creates the famous meeting between Hannibal
and the Roman general Scipio before the Battle of Zama
(202 B.C.). Scipio refuses Hannibal's plea for peace and wins
a decisive victory over the once-mighty leader.*

Hannibal was the first to speak, after the usual
salutation. He said that "he wished that the Romans
had never coveted any possession outside Italy, nor the
Carthaginians outside Libya; for these were both noble
empires, and were, so to speak, marked out by nature. But
since," he continued, "our rival claims to Sicily first made
us enemies, and then those for Iberia; and since, finally,
unwarned by the lessons of misfortune, we have gone so
far that the one nation has endangered the very soil of
its native land, and the other is now actually doing so, all
that there remains for us to do is to try our best to depre-
cate the wrath of the gods, and to put an end, as far as in

us lies, to these feelings of obstinate hostility. I personally am ready to do this, because I have learnt by actual experience that Fortune is the most fickle thing in the world, and inclines with decisive favor now to one side and now to the other on the slightest pretext, treating mankind like young children....

...But it is about you that I am anxious, Scipio. For you are still a young man, and everything has succeeded to your wishes both in Iberia and Libya, and you have as yet never experienced the ebb tide of Fortune; I fear, therefore, that my words, true as they are, will not influence you. But do look at the facts in the light of one story, and that not connected with a former generation, but our own.

Look at me! I am that Hannibal who, after the battle of Cannae, became master of nearly all Italy; and presently advancing to Rome itself, and pitching my camp within forty stades of it, deliberated as to what I should do with you and your country; but now I am in Libya debating with you, a Roman, as to the bare existence of myself and my countrymen. With such a reverse as that before your eyes, I beg you not to entertain high thoughts, but to deliberate with a due sense of human weakness on the situation; and the way to do that is among good things to choose the greatest, among evils the least.

What man of sense, then, would deliberately choose to incur the risk which is now before you. If you conquer, you will add nothing of importance to your glory or to that of your country; while, if you are worsted, you will have been yourself the means of entirely cancelling all the honors and glories you have already won. What then is the point that I am seeking to establish by these arguments? It is that the Romans should retain all the countries for which we have hitherto contended——I mean Sicily, Sardinia, and Iberia; and that the Carthaginians should engage never to go to war with Rome for these; and also that all the islands lying between Italy and Libya should belong to Rome. For I am persuaded that such a treaty will be at once safest for the Carthaginians, and most glorious for you and the entire people of Rome."

In reply to this speech of Hannibal, Scipio said "That neither in the Sicilian nor Iberian war were the Romans the aggressors, but notoriously the Carthaginians, which no one knew better than Hannibal himself."

*Source:* Polybius, *The Histories*, trans. by Evelyn S. Shuckburgh (London: Macmillan and Co., 1889).

# PROJECT IDEAS

Now you have read a modern biography of Hannibal, as well as writings about him from ancient times. Use the evidence you have gathered to complete one or more of these projects.

## Defending Hannibal

It is said that history is written by the victors. Much of Hannibal's history was written by his archenemies, the Romans. With this in mind, prepare a speech in which you defend Hannibal against charges of wickedness. Your arguments must be based on facts, but your goal is to persuade. Consider the following points:

- The humiliation of Carthage after the First Punic War

- How Hannibal was indoctrinated as a child to hate the Romans

- Hannibal's attempts to spare his homeland from a Roman invasion

- His genius as a military commander

- His attempt to make peace with Scipio

- His behavior in the context of his time

## Interpret an Ancient Reading

In *The Histories*, Polybius describes the meeting between Hannibal and Scipio. According to Polybius, Hannibal advances several arguments as to why Scipio should accept a peace. Rewrite this text for a contemporary audience. What specific reasons and advice does Hannibal offer Scipio?

## Wicked Tweets

Create two or three tweets from Hannibal about important events in his life. These might include his trek across the Alps or his ingenious military tactics. Be sure to limit your tweets to 140 characters and include hashtags.

Here's an example: Hey, Romans, I'm over here! No, wait, I'm over there! I am one step ahead and full of surprises! Better look out or I'll ensnare you in my pincer! @HannibalAdPortus #ElephantsOvertheAlps

# Fabius

(?–203 B.C.)

Quintus Fabius Maximus was a Roman politician. He was made dictator after Rome's defeat at Lake Trasimene in 217 B.C. Fabius pursued a cautious and defensive strategy against Carthage, earning him the nickname "The Delayer." His strategy avoided the fierce battle that Hannibal had hoped would lead to Rome's surrender.

# Flaminius

(?–217 B.C.)

Flaminius was a Roman politician and military leader. As commander of the Roman legions in 217 B.C., Flaminius tried to prevent Hannibal and his armies from advancing on Rome. But on the battlefield near Lake Trasimene, in a morning fog, Hannibal's armies ambushed the Romans. Flaminius and 15,000 Roman soldiers were killed.

# Hamilcar Barca

(?–228 B.C.)

Hamilcar Barca was a Carthaginian general and the father of Hannibal, Hasdrubal, and Mago Barca. In 247 B.C., Hamilcar invaded Sicily, where he fought the Romans until Carthage's defeat in the First Punic War in 241 B.C. Around 238 B.C. he began the conquest of Iberia, drowning there in battle in 228 B.C.

# Hanno
(?–?)

Hanno was a Carthaginian senator and a leading opponent of Hannibal. He blamed Hannibal for inciting the Second Punic War (218–201 B.C.). Hannibal's attack on Saguntum, an Iberian city allied with Rome, had angered the Romans.

# Hasdrubal the Fair
(?–221 B.C.)

Hasdrubal the Fair was a Carthaginian general and Hamilcar Barca's son-in-law. When Hamilcar died in 228 B.C., Hasdrubal took command of Carthage's army. He used diplomacy to build Carthaginian power and wealth in Iberia. He also founded the city of New Carthage there. He was assassinated in 221 B.C.

# Hasdrubal Barca
(?–207 B.C.)

Hasdrubal Barca was a Carthaginian general, the son of Hamilcar Barca and brother of Hannibal and Mago. In 208 B.C. the Romans defeated Hasdrubal's army in Iberia. Hasdrubal took his troops over the Alps and into Italy, intending to join Hannibal there. But he was attacked by Roman armies and killed in 207 B.C.

## Mago Barca
(?–c. 203 B.C.)

Mago Barca was a Carthaginian general, the son of Hamilcar Barca and the brother of Hannibal and Hasdrubal. Mago fought bravely at the Battle of Trebia in Italy in 218 B.C., helping Hannibal defeat the Romans there. But in 203 B.C., Mago was defeated in battle as he was bringing soldiers to Hannibal.

## Maharbal
(?–? B.C.)

Maharbal was a Carthaginian who commanded Hannibal's Numidian cavalry in the Second Punic War (218–201 B.C.). His military skills were vital to Hannibal's early victories in Italy. He is also famous for questioning Hannibal's reluctance to besiege Rome after Hannibal's great victory over the Romans at Cannae in Italy in 216 B.C.

## Publius Cornelius Scipio
(?–211 B.C.)

Scipio was a Roman politician and general and the father of Scipio Africanus. In 218 B.C. Scipio commanded the Roman armies along with his co-consul Sempronius. In Italy, Scipio survived a skirmish with Hannibal at the Ticinus River. Soon after, the Roman armies, this time led by Sempronius, were defeated at the Battle of Trebia.

# Publius Cornelius Scipio Africanus
## (c. 236–183 B.C.)

The younger Scipio was a Roman politician and general. In 204 B.C. Scipio's legions invaded North Africa and marched toward Carthage. There, in 202 B.C., Scipio refused Carthage's peace offer and defeated Hannibal's armies at the Battle of Zama, the last great battle of the Second Punic War (218–201 B.C.). In honor of this victory he was given the surname Africanus.

# Varro
## (?–? B.C.)

Varro was a Roman politician and military leader. Commanding Rome's legions in the spring of 216 B.C., Varro faced Hannibal in Italy at the Battle of Cannae with one of the largest armies ever to take the field. Varro lost the battle when Hannibal's forces surrounded his armies and slaughtered 50,000 Romans.

# Timeline of Terror

**247:** Hannibal is born in Carthage.

**238:** Hannibal accompanies his father, Hamilcar, as he attempts to conquer Iberia for Carthage.

**221:** Hasdrubal is assassinated by a Celt; Hannibal takes command.

**217:** Hannibal defeats the Romans at Lake Trasimene.

**212:** Carthage takes port city of Tarentum.

**247**

**228:** Hamilcar is killed in battle; Hasdrubal the Fair becomes commander of Carthage's army.

**216:** Hannibal's ambush leads to a huge victory at Cannae.

**241:** Rome defeats Carthage in the First Punic War.

**218:** Hannibal attacks Saguntum. Rome declares war on Carthage, launching the Second Punic War. Hannibal forces a Roman retreat at the Ticinus River and defeats the Romans at the Battle of Trebia.

**206:** Scipio conquers Iberia for Rome.

**201:** Carthage accepts harsh Roman terms, ending the Second Punic War.

**204:** Scipio lands in Africa and defeats the Carthaginian forces in two battles.

**183:** With Romans closing in, Hannibal dies after drinking poison.

**203:** Mago is defeated in Italy while attempting to bring soldiers to his brother Hannibal. Hannibal returns to Carthage.

183

**207:** Hasdrubal Barca, Hannibal's younger brother, is killed in battle while attempting to bring soldiers to Hannibal.

**c. 195:** Under threat of arrest, Hannibal flees Carthage.

**202:** Hannibal is defeated by Scipio at the Battle of Zama.

**211:** Hoping to draw Roman forces away from their siege of Capua, Hannibal camps outside Rome.

# GLOSSARY

**agile** (AJ-il) *adjective* able to move quickly and easily

**allied** (AL-ide) *adjective* working together for a common cause

**ambassador** (am-BASS-uh-dur) *noun* the top person sent by a government to represent it in another country or region

**archenemy** (arch-EN-uh-mee) *noun* a person's worst enemy

**battering ram** (BAT-ur-ing RAM) *noun* a large wooden beam with a steel head that was used to break down city walls in ancient times

**bridle** (BRYE-duhl) *noun* the straps that fit around a horse's head and mouth are used to control the horse

**catapult** (CAT-uh-puhlt) *noun* a huge weapon, similar to a large slingshot, used for firing rocks over castle walls

**cavalry** (KAV-uhl-ree) *noun* soldiers who ride on horseback

**chieftain** (CHEEF-tuhn) *noun* the leader of a tribe, clan, or community

**consul** (KON-suhl) *noun* in the Roman Republic, a leader elected by a military assembly to head the Roman government and command the army in times of war; two consuls served at a time and could cancel each other's decisions

**corpse** (KORPS) *noun* a dead body

**corruption** (kuh-RUHP-shun) *noun* the misuse of public office for private gain

**decapitate** (dee-KAP-uh-tayt) *verb* to cut a person's head off

**delegation** (del-uh-GAY-shuhn) *noun* a group of people that represents an organization or a government at meetings

**determination** (di-TUR-min-AY-shun) *noun* the act of deciding definitely and firmly

**detestation** (dee-test-AY-shun) *noun* extreme hatred or dislike

**dictator** (DIK-tay-tur) *noun* in the Roman Republic, a leader with unlimited power; in times of crisis the Senate could ask for the consuls to nominate a dictator for a six-month term

**diplomacy** (di-PLOH-muh-see) *noun* the act of dealing with people using words instead of violence

**empire** (EM-pire) *noun* a group of regions that have the same ruler

**ferocity** (fuh-RAH-si-tee) *noun* the state or quality of being eagerly violent

**guerrilla** (guh-RIL-uh) *adjective* made up of a small group of fighters that may launch surprise attacks against larger forces

**haggard** (HAG-urd) *adjective* appearing thin, tired, and worried

**infantry** (IN-fuhn-tree) *noun* the part of an army that fights on foot

**javelin** (JAV-uh-luhn) *noun* a heavy throwing spear with a six-foot iron shaft

**legion** (LEE-juhn) *noun* in the Roman Republic, a military unit consisting of 4,200 foot soldiers, each armed with a short sword and two javelins

**prophesy** (PROF-uh-see) *verb* to predict the future

**ravage** (RAV-uhj) *verb* to completely destroy a wide area

**resolve** (ri-ZOLV) *noun* firm determination to do something

**revere** (ri-VEER) *verb* to feel deep respect or admiration for someone or something

**senate** (SEN-it) *noun* a body of officials elected to make laws

**slinger** (SLING-uhr) *noun* a person who is skilled at using a sling, a loop of leather used for throwing stones

**strait** (STRAYT) *noun* a narrow strip of water that connects two larger bodies of water

# FIND OUT MORE

*Here are some books with more information about Hannibal.*

## NONFICTION

Abbott, Jacob. *Hannibal: Makers of History.* N. Charleston, SC: CreateSpace Independent Publishing, 2013. (214 pages)
*A vintage biography, edited and brought up to date for readers aged twelve and up.*

Brocklehurst, Ruth. *The Roman Army.* Lake Hopatcong, NJ: Usborne, 2003. (48 pages)
*Explores how an efficient, highly trained army helped build and run the Roman Empire.*

Green, Robert. *Hannibal* (First Books). New York: Franklin Watts, 1997. (64 pages)
*This engaging book explores the life of one of ancient history's greatest military commanders.*

Mills, Cliff. *Hannibal* (Ancient World Leaders). New York: Chelsea House, 2008. (128 pages)
*An easy-to-read biography of Hannibal.*

Nardo, Don. *The Punic Wars.* San Diego, CA: Lucent Books, 1996. (111 pages)
*This excellent, clearly written book on the Punic Wars includes primary-source materials.*

O'Connell, Robert L. *The Ghosts of Cannae: Hannibal and the Darkest Hour of the Roman Republic.* New York: Random House, 2010. (310 pages)
*Focuses on Hannibal and his Roman nemesis Scipio Africanus, a rivalry that led to the slaughter at Cannae.*

Price, Sean. *Hannibal of Carthage* (Hero Journals). Chicago, IL: Raintree, 2013. (48 pages)
*Major events of Hannibal's life, written as conversational, first-person journal entries.*